HAL·LEONARD

WEDDING ESSENTIALS

INCLUDES REFERENCE CD

SERVICE MUSIC FOR WEDDINGS

ISBN 978-1-4234-8864-4

HAL·LEONARD® CORPORATION

7777 W. BLUEMOUND RD. P.O. BOX 13819 MILWAUKEE, WI 53213

In Australia Contact:
Hal Leonard Australia Pty. Ltd.
4 Lentara Court
Cheltenham, Victoria, 3192 Australia
Email: ausadmin@halleonard.com.au

Visit Hal Leonard Online at
www.halleonard.com

CANON IN D

By JOHANN PACHELBEL

Adagio

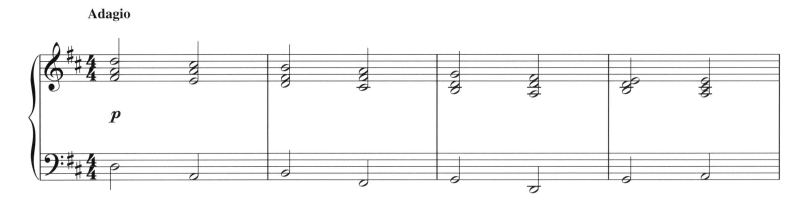

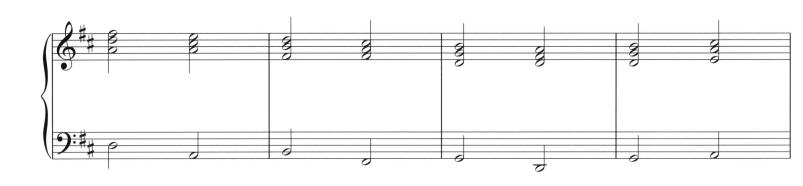

6

JESU, JOY OF MAN'S DESIRING

By JOHANN SEBASTIAN BACH

Moderato

JUPITER
(Chorale Theme)
from THE PLANETS

By GUSTAV HOLST

TRUMPET VOLUNTARY

By JEREMIAH CLARKE

Andante con moto

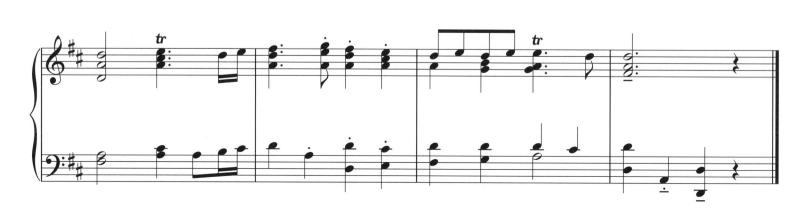

AMAZING GRACE

Words by JOHN NEWTON
Traditional American Melody

Flowing

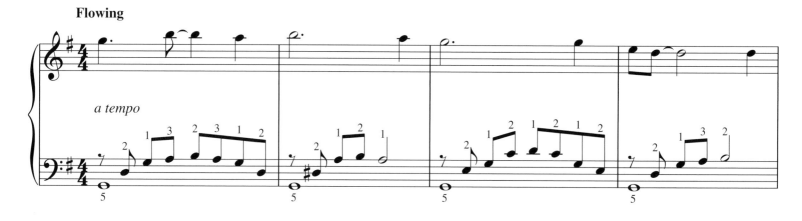

Decisively

molto rit.　　　*cresc.*　　　***ff***

O PERFECT LOVE

Words by DOROTHY FRANCES GURNEY
Music by JOSEPH BARNBY

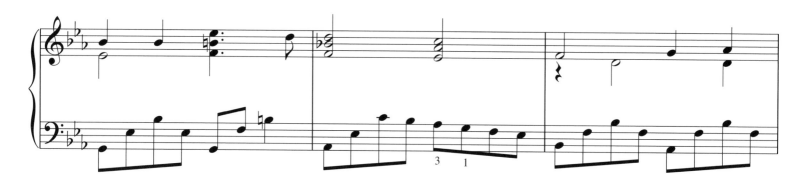

AVE MARIA

By FRANZ SCHUBERT

Molto lento

ALLEGRO MAESTOSO
from WATER MUSIC

By GEORGE FRIDERIC HANDEL

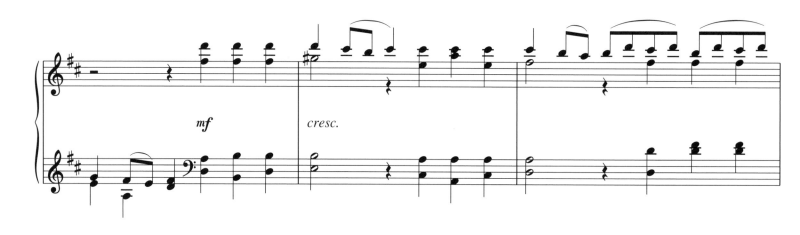

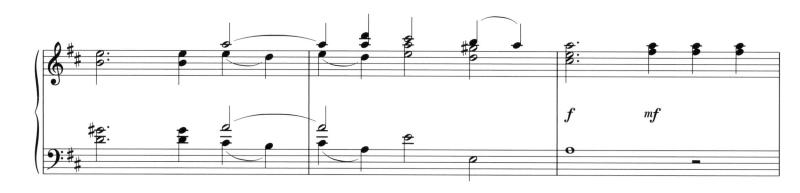

ODE TO JOY
from SYMPHONY NO. 9 IN D MINOR

By LUDWIG VAN BEETHOVEN

With spirit

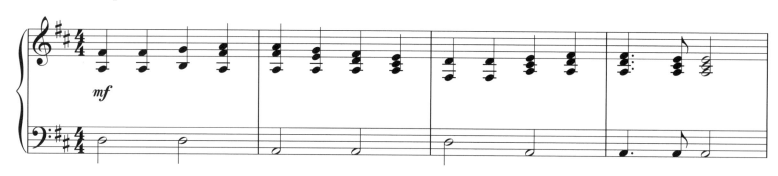

RONDEAU
Excerpt

By JEAN-JOSEPH MOURET

HAL•LEONARD WEDDING ESSENTIALS

INCLUDES REFERENCE CD

The **Wedding Essentials** series is a great resource for wedding musicians, featuring beautiful arrangements for a variety of instruments. Each book includes a reference CD to help couples choose the perfect songs for their wedding ceremony or reception.

Christian Wedding Favorites

Answered Prayer • God Causes All Things to Grow • God Knew That I Needed You • Household of Faith • I Will Be Here • If You Could See What I See • Love Will Be Our Home • Seekers of Your Heart • This Day • 'Til the End of Time.
00311941 P/V/G... $16.99

Contemporary Wedding Ballads

Beautiful in My Eyes • Bless the Broken Road • Endless Love • (Everything I Do) I Do It for You • From This Moment On • Have I Told You Lately • Here and Now • Love of a Lifetime • More Than Words • When You Say You Love Me.
00311942 P/V/G... $16.99

Love Songs for Weddings

Grow Old with Me • Here, There and Everywhere • If • Longer • Part of My Heart • Valentine • We've Only Just Begun • The Wedding Song • You and I • You Raise Me Up.
00311943 Piano Solo... $16.99

Service Music for Weddings

PROCESSIONALS, RECESSIONALS, LIGHTING OF THE UNITY CANDLE
Allegro maestoso • Amazing Grace • Ave Maria • Canon in D • Jesu, Joy of Man's Desiring • Jupiter (Chorale Theme) • O Perfect Love • Ode to Joy • Rondeau • Trumpet Voluntary.
00311944 Piano Solo... $14.99

Wedding Guitar Solos

All I Ask of You • Gabriel's Oboe • Grow Old with Me • Hallelujah • Here, There and Everywhere • More Than Words • Sunrise, Sunset • Wedding Song (There Is Love) • When I Fall in Love • You Raise Me Up.
00701335 Guitar Solo.. $16.99

Wedding Vocal Solos

Grow Old with Me • I Swear • In My Life • Longer • The Promise (I'll Never Say Goodbye) • Someone Like You • Sunrise, Sunset • Till There Was You • Time After Time • We've Only Just Begun.
00311945 High Voice... $16.99
00311946 Low Voice... $16.99

Worship for Weddings

Be Unto Your Name • Broken and Beautiful • Center • He Is Here • Here and Now • Holy Ground • How Beautiful • Listen to Our Hearts • Today (As for Me and My House).
00311949 P/V/G... $16.99

FOR MORE INFORMATION, SEE YOUR LOCAL MUSIC DEALER, OR WRITE TO:

HAL•LEONARD® CORPORATION

7777 W. BLUEMOUND RD. P.O. BOX 13819 MILWAUKEE, WI 53213

www.halleonard.com

Prices, content, and availability subject to change without notice.